Python for Beginners

The Ultimate Guide to Python Programming

Joshua Welsh

TABLE OF CONTENTS

INTRODUCTION

Congratulations on downloading Python for Beginners: The Ultimate Guide to Python Programming and thank yo u for doing so.

The following chapters will discuss the Python programming language and how to get started programming in this multifaceted language.

Choosing to learn to program, especially in the Python programming language, is one of the most vital choi ces you can make for yourself, both personally and from a career context.

Learning to program will enable you in multiple ways. First and foremost, programming is an invaluable skill set in the workforce. Not only does learning how to talk to your computer enable you to more positions in roles specifically catered to computers and programming, but it also makes you very in-demand in career fields that are outside of that scope. For example, in fields such as biology and chemistry, being able to program is a very marketable skill because it demonstrates that you're a problem solver and that you'll be able to automate parts of your work as you need to. Additionally, as technology begins to become a bigger and bigger parts of our life, there's starting to be an even greater intersection of non-computer disciplines with computer technology. Being able to program puts you in a prime position where you're at the forefront of this intersection.

On top of that, learning to program enables you to do a great more many things in your personal life. Programming as a hobby is incredibly rewarding. You can program video games, create mods for already -existent video games, create applications to automate certain processes - the possibilities, really, are endless.

Python in particular is a fantastic choice for all of this because Python is a language which has a huge following and user base. It's arguably the most popular scripting language, seeming to outpace similar and related languages such as Ruby and Perl. The documenta tion for Python spans from proverbial wall to proverbial wall. Python can be used for anything from server-side web applications to game programming to fully fledged applications with GUIs and complete functionality.

On top of this, Python is a great langu age for learning the concepts underlying all programming because

There are plenty of books on this subject on the market, thanks again for choosing this one! Every effort was made to ensure it is full of as much useful information as possible, please enjoy!

CHAPTER 1

SETTING UP / YOUR FIRST PROGRAM

In order to do anything with the beautifully articulate Python programming language, you first have to set up an environment in which you can do things. I'd say that goes without saying, though.

You're going to need a few different things in order to get your Python setup going. Firstly, you're going to need to install Python itself or check to see if it's already installed.

Verifying the install is pretty simple. In Windows, press the Windows key and search for "Python". If it's there, it'll pop up in the list of applications. On Mac and Linux systems, open up the Terminal and try to run the command python. Your output should look a bit like this:

```
user@userpc:~$ python
Python 2.7.12 (default, Jul  1 2016, 15:12:24)
[GCC 5.4.0 20160609] on linux2
Type "help", "copyright", "credits" or
"license" for more information.
>>>
```

If this is the result you got, then perfect. If you don't have Python installed, you'll get a message that says something along the lines of "command python is invalid".

In this case, you'll need to install Python. Most full -featured desktop installations of Linux systems - be they Ubuntu, Fedora, Debian, CentOS, or any derivative of those - will most likely have Python by default. Mac OS does a s well. Windows normally does not.

Regardless, if you don't have Python, you obviously are going to need to, well, *get* Python.

The simplest way to go about this is by simply going to the Python website (python.org). From there, you go to the downloads page. For the purposes of this book, we're going to be working with Python 2.7.12. The reason that we're doing this is because almost all legacy code you'll encounter and, indeed, a lot of the code being written today, is written in Python 2. Python 3 very wel l may be the future, but it's not the current. If you run into an event where you need to work with Python 3, it's super easy to transfer your skills over to Python 3 anyway. Pay careful attention to the installation process on Windows, and if there's an o ption to create PATH variables, ensure that it's selected. PATH variables are what allow you to launch a program from the command line and perform certain actions with it.

Once you have Python installed, we're going to need to install a text editor from which we'll work with Python. You may be tempted to work with the Python IDLE, but this really isn't the best idea. It's much better to get a text editor, if only for the reason that 1) you learn the environment and can work with numerous different programmi ng languages from within it, and 2) you can grab plugins which will make your job as a programmer much easier.

Whether you're doing this for a career or a hobby, you're a programmer now. And very, very few programmers use the Python IDLE. Some prefer emacs , some prefer vim, some use Sublime Text, others use Notepad++.

For the purposes of this book, we're going to be using something called Atom. You can grab this from their website (atom.io). The reason that we're using Atom is because it's super simple to set up, can be used on any major platform, and is incredibly customizable and extensible. It's a great starting point for text editors.

If you have a friend who's trying to get you into programming and saying "no, you have to use *insert text editor here!*", then there's nothing wrong with appeasing them. Text editors are just environments to write code. But if you're new and scared of what the world of programming may hold, Atom is a very safe choice.

Anyway, you go to atom.io and just head to their downloads page and grab a copy of the software. Install it and you're ready to go.

The other reason we're not using the IDLE is because it teaches you to use a crutch. I want you to learn how to launch Python code using the command line, because it's just frankly important knowledge to have. In this way, you also need to know how to navigate and perform basic commands within the command line. In Mac and Linux, this command line is called Terminal. In Windows, you won't be using the standard command line - instead, you'll be using the PowerShell, which you can find by simply searching for PowerShell in the start menu.

If you don't have basic knowledge of file system navigation via command line, then frankly you need to learn it. It's beyond the scope of this book, a nd I'm not going to cover it in here because there's precious time to be spent teaching other things.

Create a new folder where you'd like to store your code. Then open Atom and right click the sidebar to the left. Click the object that says "Add Project F older", then choose the folder that you just created. Then left -click the project folder on the sidebar. It's now the active folder. Right click anywhere on the sidebar and click "New file".

On the dialog that says "Enter the path [...]" you can just enter a filename. We're going to call this file ch1.py. Technically, you could call it anything you like. This isn't like Java where the filename has to correspond to something in the code. But for simplicity's sake, yes, we're calling it ch1.py.

Within ch1.py, type the following:

```
print "hello world"
```

Then save the file. The shortcut for this, if you don't know it, is *Ctrl+S*.

Head back to your Terminal/PowerShell. Navigate to the folder which has the ch1.py file, then execute it by typing the following:

```
python ch1.py
```

Your output should look something along the lines of this:

```
user@userpc:~/Python$ python ch1.py

hello world
```

If that's how it came out, then awesome. You just wrote your first Python program. How proud are you? I'm pretty proud of you. Now we're going to work on some more important concepts like variables and math.

CHAPTER 2

VARIABLES, VALUES, EXPRESSIONS, AND MATH

Wordy chapter title, no? Well, these concepts are super - duper important. There's no way to really undervalue any of them, so we're going to go through them one-by-one.

The first thing you need to do for this chapter is create a new file. Call it ch2.py. This is what you're going to be working with throughout this whole chapter. We're going to do this every chapter, so just get used to that se t of instructions.

In your new file, we're going to be working with a couple of new ideas. The first of these are variables.

Variables and Values

What are variables? **Variables** are *things which store a given value*. These values can have many different forms . In languages such as Java and C++, you have to explicitly declare what type of variable you're creating.

For example, in order to declare the variable car and give it the value of "Nissan Maxima" in Java, we'd have to do something along the lines of:

```
String car = "Nissan Maxima"
```

Python makes this super simple though. We don't have to declare the type at all. We can just do this:

```
car = "Nissan Maxima"
```

Python, ever knowledgeable, knows exactly what type we want without us saying it at all. That's impress ive. It can do this because we imply that it's a string variable by the fact that its value is, well, a string.

It's important to know about types though, because there are some things you can't do. For example, if you compared the following variables:

```
num1 = 12
num2 = "12"
```

They wouldn't be the same, since num2 is a string while num1 is an integer.

What are the primary types of variables in Python? Fantastic question, my friend. These are the primary types and their definitions.

Type	Description	Declaration example
Integer	A whole number	`kindsOfCheese = 3`
Float	A decimal number	`weightOfCheese = 3.88`
Boolean	True or False	`hasCheese = True`
String	Text	`nameOfCheese = "brie"`

Super important distinctions, but Python makes it relatively easy to deal with all of these.

Go into ch2.py and create two variables. One will be called favoriteFood and the other will be called days. For favoriteFood, set it to be a string which states your favorite food. days should be an integer with a number that y ou make up.

My example looks like this:

```
favoriteFood = "thai
curry" days = 40
```

Now let's print our favorite food to the console and tell the world!

```
print "My favorite food is %s." % favoriteFood
```

We'll talk more about what exactly our print command just now meant in the next chapter. In the meantime, though, let's talk about variables and how they can change.

Operators

After your print statement, you need to change the value of your favorite food. Go ahead and make it your second favorite food. Your code should then look a little like this:

```
favoriteFood = "thai
curry" days = 40
print "My favorite food is %s." %
favoriteFood favoriteFood = "pizza"
```

Now let's add another print statement and make sense of all of this.

```
print "Wait, never mind! I ate that %d days
in a row. I'm sick of it. My favorite food is
now %s." % (days, favoriteFood)
```

Save and execute again. You should see that the favoriteFood variable changed on the second instance! Crazy.

That's because you just used an *assignment operator*. Assignment operators are one of several different types of operators in Python which can be used to deal with values.

= is the simplest one, and just means that variable x takes the value of variable y, like so.

x = y

There are a few other assignment operators t oo. Here's the full list:

Operator	Example	Meaning
=	x = y	x is y
+=	x += y	x = x + y
-=	x -= y	x = x - y
*=	x *= y	x = x * y
/=	x /= y	x = x / y
%=	x %= y	x = x % y
**=	x **= y	x = x ** y
//=	x //= y	x = x // y

Some of these don't make sense, but they will in a second. The point to drive home here is that these are massively important and useful. For example, you can use them in order to increment. Consider the following example:

```
i = 3
# i is 3, but we want to add one to
it. i += 1
# The underlying arithmetic is i = i + 1.
```

```
#Substituting variables for their value: i =
3 + 1
# So, i is now 4.
```

These build upon what are called the arithmetic operators.
These are easy to grasp.

Operator	Name	Function
+	Addition	Adds values together.
-	Subtraction	Subtracts a value from another.
*	Multiplication	Multiplies values.
/	Division	Divides values.
%	Modulo	Gives remainder. (7 % 2 = 1)
**	Exponentiation	Denotes exponent. (2**2 = 4)
//	Floor division	Floor division.

There's one more type of operator that we're going to
discuss, and we're actually going to discuss it while

discussing the broader concept of expressions.

Expressions

We've talked about how things can have an inherent true -or-false value, right? You may remember from high school or college math working with something called *expressions*. These were different from equations, in that they weren't meant to be evaluated. They were simply true or false. Ringing any bells? Anyway, Python - and programming languages in general - accomodate for expressions. In fact, they don't only *accommodate* them, but they provide for them, and quite handily at that. Expressions provide for a portion of programming known as *control flow*, which is crucial. Programs often aren't linear. There are a ton of decisions to be made in the writing and execution of a program, and there will be situations where you certainly have to make different decisions based upon a piece of data.

There are a very different ways to do this. The most general way is with something called a conditional operator. These provide ways to compare two different values.

Here are the primary conditional operators:

Operator	Meaning
x == y	x is equal to y
x != y	x is not equal to y
x <= y	x is less than or equal to y
x >= y	x is greater than or equal to y

x < y	x is less than y
x > y	x is greater than y

You can also store these to variables. That's because all these expressions do is evaluate themselves and then return True or False. So you may have an expression, but all that value represents is a single True or False. Like this:

```
votesForCat = 4
votesForDog = 5
dogsWin = votesForCat < votesForDog
print "Do dogs win? %r" % dogsWin
```

If you coded this, the output would be along the lines of:

```
Do dogs win? True
```

So our variable "dogsWin" evaluates the expression of "votesForCat are less than votesForDog" and returns whether it's true or false, then stores that.

This is a really big part of the upcoming lesson on conditionals. There are numerous aspects which make this a very relevant and important lesson to learn, but regardless of the numerous "why"s, the lesson to take home is that this is one of the more central and core concepts of programming: comparing variables to one another and making a decision based off of that information.

In the following chapter, we're going to work on some more exact and dedicated examples of this phenomenon.

CHAPTER 3

CONDITIONALS

As I've said before, the notion of comparing values and making a decision is incredibly integral to the entire field and subject of computer programming. Computers, at their cores, are just ones and zeroes. Bits constantly being compared, moved around, chang ed, all of that. The ability to take these and compare them to one another and make a decision opens up so many possibilities.

There's one major way to do this in Python. This is through the use of something called an if statement.

An **if statement** can be defined as a chunk of code which looks at an expression, evaluates, and then takes action if that expression is true.

Potential conditionals

The first thing we're going to cover are the simplest form of if statements. I call these potential conditionals, be cause no code is guaranteed to be ran unless the expression works out to be true.

Create a new file called ch3.py. We're going to go ahead and type the following code within it, which is coincidentally an insight into the mind of a six-year-old:

```
bananas = 6
fireTruck = "red"
if bananas == 0:
print "Uh oh, something went wrong - I
don't have any bananas!"
print "Did you know fire trucks are %s?"
% fireTruck
```

Execute and run the code. Your output should be something along the lines of this:

```
user@userpc:~/Python$ python ch3.py
Did you know fire trucks are red?
```

Why do you think that it didn't output the string before? Yes, the answer is as obvious as you think.

First, it looked at the expression:

```
if bananas == 0
```
Then it parsed it into its values:
```
if 6 == 0
```

This is clearly not true, so the code following it wasn't executed. Easy peasy.

But wait, what if we want to see if something is *not* true? Well, this is where there's actually another conditional operator that we need to cover. This one is called the negative operator. Let's go ahead and change the if statement to look like this:

```
if not bananas == 0:
print "Wow, I have bananas!"
```

Now run your program again. The output should look like this:

```
user@userpc:~/Python$ python
ch3.py Wow, I have bananas!
Did you know fire trucks are red?
```

Perfect. We now know we have bananas. There's also another way to evaluate this, though. Remember the inequality operator? We could also easily have typed:

```
if bananas != 0:
print "Wow, I have bananas!"
```

When doing mathematical comparisons, it's generally not useful to use this. But for boolean expressions, it's really useful. For example, if we had this chunk of code:

```
hasBananas = True
if not hasBananas:
print "I don't have any bananas!"
```

It'd work great. You don't actually have to write out

```
if hasBananas != True
```

or

```
if hasBananas == False
```

The important thing to drive home here is that boolean conditionals are very simple and since expressions innately check for being either true or false, since booleans have an *innate* veracity, you don't have to compare one veracity against another. All veracity is constant, and if the boolean variable is "true", then it's "true". Full stop. The conditional operation will realize such. Philosophical, right?

Anyhow, all the *not* operator does is check to see if the following expression is *true* instead of *false*. This can be very useful though, and it's important that you learn and remember it.

Absolute conditionals

But what if you want a block of code that checks a condition and still does something, even if it's not true?

Let's just erase the code we have in ch3.py so far, we're going to redo some of this.

The first thing we want to do is ask how many bananas the person has. But we also want to store this to a variable. How can we do this?

Well, first we have to create the variable:

```
bananas =
```

And then we have to figure out how to retrieve the information. In Python 2, we do this using a method called raw_input(). This is *not* to be confused with input(). input() allows the user to enter Python code and it's overall just a huge security risk to leave that kind of access to your code exposed, so we're going to avoid that altogether.

raw_input() also has a handy feature which allows you to print out text alongside of it. This simplifies a chunk of code like:

```
print "How old are
you?" age = raw_input()
```

so that it's just more along the lines of

```
age = raw_input("How old are you?")
```

Note the way that the raw_input function works, too! We'll talk about return values when we talk about methods, but this method returns a *string*, which means that whatever variable is assigned the value of raw_input() is ultimately

16

going to be a string.

Anyway, so now we know how we can to the banana code. Write in your now empty code template this line of code:

```
bananas = raw_input("How many bananas do
I have?\n")
```

Perfectly simple. We now have a variable called bananas which carries a string of whatever the user entered. Great start.

Now we're going to start working on the chunk of code.

Let's assume we want to juggle ba nanas. If we only have 1, we obviously can't juggle the bananas, right? So we want to make that clear. Let's make an if statement!

```
if bananas == 1:
print "I can't juggle these bananas, I
only have one!"
```

But wait... if you run this, you'll get an error. Why? Because *bananas* is currently a string data type. We have to turn it into an integer. How do we do those?

This is called *casting*, and Python actually makes it relatively straightforward. What you do is you name the type that you want to cast to, then in parentheses the variable you're trying to convert to that type. If you wanted to turn a string into an integer, you'd do this:

```
int(string)
```

That's exactly what we want to do here. So let's work with that. Above your if-statement, let's turn bananas into an integer. Your code should now look like this:

```
bananas = raw_input("How many bananas do
I have?\n")
bananas = int(bananas)
if bananas == 1:
print "I can't juggle these bananas, I
only have one!"
```

So far, so good. If you'd like, you can test this out by runn ing it and entering 1 when prompted for the number of bananas. It should output the text "I can't juggle these bananas, I only have one." Complex stuff. Anyhow, we have to implement a safety, though. This is where the *absolute* cause of absolute conditions comes from. Absolute conditions ensure that code will be run no matter what happens. These are otherwise called if else statements.

```
If (condition) is true (
)
otherwise, do this (
)
```

Both absolute and potential conditions deal with what happens *if* a condition is true, but only absolute conditions deal with what happens if they *aren't* true. Let's modify our code a bit.

```
if bananas == 1:
print "I can't juggle these bananas, I
only have one!"
else:
print "Juggling has commenced. Viva
la révolucion."
```

Save your code and run it and try putting something other than 1. It should say "juggling has commenced" and then call for the jugglers of the world to unite. However, what if we had 0 bananas? It still says that. But you can't juggle 0 bananas. This is a paradox, and I'm no longer satisfied with the state of the code. We need to add something else to this...

we need to check for another condition. "How can we go about doing that?" you ask? It's impossibly simple, actually! We use what's called an *else if statement*. So let's fix this code right quick, and add a stipulation for if bananas are 0.

```
if bananas == 1:
print "I can't juggle these bananas, I only
have one!"
elif bananas == 0:
print "I have 0 bananas. I urgently need
bananas before juggling."
else:
print "Juggling has commenced. Viva
la révolucion."
```

There we go. That's perfect! Save this chunk of code and run it, let's see what we can get out of it. Test it out by entering different values. It should change depending on whether you put it 0, 1, or anything else.

CHAPTER 4

STRING FORMATTING AND ESCAPE SEQUENCES

I mentioned earlier that I was going to explain at a later point what exactly is going on with the print statements I was using. The explanation is relatively simple, but a bit more nuanced and difficult to grasp entirely.

Basically, what we were using was a formatted print statement. These mean that you give it a string to output, which is formatted with other variables. This is the cleanest and best way to print strings, regardless of how you're doing them, and is considered best practice far and wide.

Go ahead and create a new file called ch4.py. Within this we're going to create a couple of variables. Let's create a variable called dogs and give it the value of 3, a variable called cats and give it the value of 4, a variable called horses given the value of 0, and a variable called frogs with the value of 1. It should look like this:

```
cats = 3
dogs = 4
cows = 0
sheep = 1
pigs = 3
```

Now let's print out what we have.

```
print "I have %d cats, and I also have
%d dogs." % (cats, dogs)
print "I have %d cows,\n%d sheep,\nand
%d pigs." % (cows, sheep, pigs)
```

```
print "That means I have:\n\t%d livestock."
% (cows + sheep + pigs)
```

Save this and run it. Your output should look a bit like this:

```
user@userpc:~/Python$ python ch4.py
I have 3 cats, and I also have 4
dogs. I have 0 cows,
1 sheep,
and 3 pigs.
That means I have:
4 livestock.
```

Super simple, right? Let's break this down part by part and see how we got from that code up there to what we have in the console.

Formatting Sequences

So, in a formatted string, you have several different ways to print out information. A formatted string has to actually convert all of the data to a string so that it can be printed out, and we tell it where we have data we want to inse rt by way of something called *formatting sequences*.

Here are the primary formatting sequences and their meaning.

Sequence	Meaning
%d	Base 10 integer. Most ordinary whole numbers.
%f	Floating point number.
%xf	Float, decimal cutoff. 9,9955: %2f = 9.99, %3f = 9.995
%r	Raw data. Normally used for debugging, not release.
%s	String.

Go back and look at the code we had and see if you can connect the dots and see why and where we used each one. There are more, but these are the ones you need to know as a beginner.

"But wait, what about the weird \n and \t things?"

Escape Sequences

Oh, you thought I'd forget about those? No way. Those are called *escape sequences*. What they basically mean is that the character after the backslash (\) doesn't mean what it normally does. \n, for example, means to move to a new line. \t means to tab over. You don't really need a chart for this, it's rather self-explanatory. There are more, but those are the primary ones. There's only one more class you need to know at this point in your programming career, and those are the punctuation escape sequences.

See, there may be times in your code where you really need to use a quotation mark or a backslash. Maybe you're quoting someone or telling a story, or teaching programming concepts like escape sequences *through* a program. Either way, if you just throw in a straight -up quotation mark or backslash, it's gonna throw things off. You have to denote specifically that you want to print these characters by using an escape sequence. \" would give you a quotation mark, \' would give you a single quotation mark, and \\ would give you a backslash.

With all of that said, it's time to move onto a much heavier and more important concept: data sets. You're going to learn what they are and how to manipulate them in the upcoming chapter.

CHAPTER 5

DATA SETS

It's that time now: you have to learn about data sets. You're growing up so fast! These are essential to understanding the other important part of control flow aside from conditional statements: loops. Loops are more often than not used to iterate through either a list or a set of data, so we may as well cover our bases and talk about data sets first.

There are a few different kinds of data sets, but the two most important ones to know in Python ar e *lists* and *dictionaries*. Are there others? Sure. Are they far more esoteric? Definitely. This will cover the bases for what you need to know, certainly. Let's start out with lists.

Lists

Okay, it's storytime. This will become more relevant later when we talk about string manipulation and string methods. Once upon a time, there was a language called C. C became extremely popular, and with it popularized the concept of data arrays. C-style data arrays set the standard for what would become the basis of lists and sets in any given language following.

The basic idea behind data arrays is that you often have data that you want to group together. Let's say you have 5 different grades for students. You wouldn't want to type this:

```
int student1Grade = 44;
int student2Grade = 96;
int student3Grade = 73;
int student4Grade = 89;
int student5Grade = 100;
```

For one, that's tedious. Secondly, that's hard to keep up with when you have a lot of them. Plus, there's the chance that you make a typo somewhere and have to fi gure it out later, and it's just a whole mess. Besides, they're all grades. Why *wouldn't* you keep them together?

Arrays simplified that. They could declare an array like this:

```
int grades[5] = { 44, 96, 73, 89, 100 };
```

This bundled all of the grades toget her into one set of data. If you wanted to change the first grade in the array, you'd just go

```
grades[0] = 45; // 0 because computers
start counting from 0, not 1.
```

See how much simpler and less complicated that is? It also allowed for things like sorting a lgorithms, which we won't cover in this book. When data is grouped together in a way like that, you're able to iterate through it and compare different objects in it.

Anyway, that's the gist of that.

This set the stage for *lists* in Python. *Arrays* have a set amount of data they can hold, and a fixed type for all of that data. Lists in Python are better than arrays for two reasons:

1) They automatically readjust their size depending upon how many elements they have.
2) You can have multiple types within a set of da ta.

24

The second is especially useful when you're dealing with parent and child classes (as we'll discuss later) and want to put both types in the same list.

Lists in Python are easy enough to declare. Let's take the former grades example. If you wanted to create a list that inhabited all of those grades, you could do it in one fell swoop:

```
grades = [44, 96, 73, 89, 100]
```

Perfect. If we wanted to print out the 2nd grade from the list, we'd just type the following:

```
print grades[1]
```

See? An absolute piece of cake. But what if you got a surprise late assignment? We can add a grade to that list incredibly simply using the *append*() method:

```
grades.append(45) # half credit for being
a slacker.
```

We can verify that we actually added the variable by printing the sixth item of the list.

```
print grades[5]
```

This would print out 45. Simple enough.

Now, to remove an element from a list is likewise very simple. There are two different ways. The pop() method returns the value, which often isn't what you want. Instead, there's the *del* keyword, which will straight up remove the element from the list.

25

For example, if you printed out the *grades* list, as it stands, you'd see this:

```
>>> grades
{ 44, 96, 73, 89, 100, 45 }
```

Let's say the person responsible for the 44 dropped the course. We could delete their grade like so:

```
del grades[0]
```

If we tried printing the grades list again, it'd look like this:

```
>>> grades
{96, 73, 89, 100, 45 }
```

Now the results are looking a little bit better, no?

But surely there's a way to improve upon t his. Right now, we can't search by student name to see who had what grade! This is where *dictionaries* come into play.

Dictionaries

The name of dictionaries come from, believe it or not, real dictionaries. Think about it. You look up a word in a dictionary and you find a definition. Dictionaries in Python, and most programming languages really, work very similarly. Dictionaries are essentially a map and key interface. You give a set of keys, which map to a given value. Simple enough, right? Let's go back to our grade example.

Let's say we wanted to a grade to every student for a given assignment, and then reference their grade by name. Create a new file called ch5.py. What we're going to do in this first is create a new dictionary called assignment1Grades. Th e keys are going to be the student names, and they're going to map to a certain value - here, of course, being their grades on the proverbial assignment one.

Great. So, let's get started. Let's say we had a student named Jack Duke who made a 44, a student named Jacob Green who made a 68, a student named Kevin Thomas who made a 99, and a student named Brad Smith who made a 73. The way we'd declare that dictionary is like so:

```
assignment1Grades = { "Jack Duke" : 44, "Jacob
Green" : 68, "Kevin Thomas" : 99, "Brad Smith"
: 73}
```

See what's happening here? The respective strings for their names are acting as keys to the given values.

After that, let's go ahead and prompt the user for which grade they'd like to pull up.

```
userIn = raw_input("What grade would you like
to pull up?\n")
```

Now we check to see if the string they entered is even in the data set. This is super easy in Python. In other languages, you'd have to iterate through the whole data set with a loop, but Python just lets you straight up see if it's in th ere or not, using the aptly named *in* keyword. This happens like so:

```
if userIn in assignment1Grades: # the beauty
of technology!
print assignment1Grades[userIn]
else:
print "That's not a valid name."
```

Notice how we fetched the value mapped to the key represented by the userIn value. Save this and test it by entering student names and then things that aren't there at all. It should print out the grades mapped to the names if you enter a proper name or tell you the name is invalid otherwise.

A lot of places uses a keymap system very similar to this. Think of grocery stores, where every item has a SKU number or a UPC code that is linked to it. You can actually reverse search an item by SKU to find the exact model. It's super impressive, and a real-world application of this technology so you don't find yourself thinking "when will I ever use this?"

Anyhow, that covers the two main data sets in Python. Now it's time to talk about how we can iterate through them with loops.

CHAPTER 6

LOOPS

Loops are a major part of programming and control flow. In fact, I'd argue they're by far one of the biggest parts. Most programs will demand utilization of a loop in one way or another. Loops, especially to a novice programmer, may sound silly. Time will show you, however, th e numerous uses and applications for the various sorts of loops.

There are two different kinds of loops in Python: *while* and *for*. *For* loops are the most important, so I'm going to spend the most time talking about them. For now, let's talk about *while* loops.

While

While loops are loops which occur while a condition is true. For as long as that value holds true, the loop will continue to execute.

The first use which springs to mind for this sort of loop is what's called a "game loop". Game loops are comprise d of two parts: a boolean which basically says whether or not the program is running/the user has chosen to quit, and a while loop which runs a given set of code for as long as the user hasn't stated they'd want to quit. Create a new file called ch6 - 1.py.

In this, create a variable called run and set it to True, and then create a variable called total and set it to 0.

Below that, we want to create a while loop. We could say *while run == True*, but as we learned earlier, that's redundant. We're just going to say this instead:

```
while run:
```

There we go, nice and clean.

Now we're going to print the total and have the user enter a number to add to it.

```
userIn = raw_input("\n\n\nCurrent total
is: %d.\nEnter a number, or anything else
to exit.\n" % total)
```

Now we're going to check to see what they entered. String objects have built-in things called methods - most objects do, in fact. There's a very handy method for this exact purpose called **string**.*isdigit()*. So let's say that if the string the user entered is a digit, we add it to total. Otherwise, we leave the loop.

First, we construct the first part of the if statement:

```
if userIn.isdigit():
```

Then we need to code what happens. First, we take total, then we have to add to it what the user entered. But before we do that, we have to convert the string the user entered into an int. Here's how I did it:

```
total += int(userIn)
```

In the else statement, we need to exit the loop. Since the loop is running for as long as the condition is true, the condition here being "while the variable *run* is set to *True*", we just have to negate that condition by setting run to false.

```
else:
print "\nGoodbye!\n" # a goodbye message --
we aren't monsters
run = False
```

By the end, your code should look along the lines of this:

```
run = True
total = 0
while run:
userIn = raw_input("\n\n\nCurrent total
is: %d.\nEnter a number, or anything else
to exit.\n" % total)
if userIn.isdigit():
total += int(userIn)
else:
print "\nGoodbye!\n!"
run = False
```

Super easy. Save that and run it and test it out. For me, it looked like this:

```
user@userpc:~/Python/book 3$ python ch6-
1.py Current total is: 0.
Enter a number, or anything else to
exit. 3
Current total is: 3.
Enter a number, or anything else to
exit. 9
Current total is: 12.
Enter a number, or anything else to
exit. fl
Goodbye!
```

Flawless and functional. True innovation. Anyway, that's pretty simple and approachable, right? Now onto the fun part: for loops.

For loops

In ye olden days of computer programming, for loops were very different from they are in Python. Then, they had three parameters: the iterator variable's starting value, the condition of the loop, and the iteration equation.

For example, if you had an array of 5 values - let's go back to the old example and call the array *grades* - and you wanted to print all of them in Java, it'd be something like this:

```
for (int i = 0; i < grades.length; i++)
{ System.out.println(i);
}
```

Python, as it tends to do, massively simplifies this. It recognizes that most for loops are used for iterating through sets of data and gears itself towards that. Let's take that same data set that we were just talking about, and iterate through in Python:

```
for i in
grades: print i
```

"i" here is the iterator variable, and can assume the form of whatever data type is in the data set. That i s to say that if you made a type called animal, and you had a set of the animal type, and every member of the animal type had a method called sleep(), then you could do this:

```
for i in animalList:
i.sleep()
```

It's important to note that the iterator name can be anything though - it certainly does *not* have to be "i". A common example that may trip you up later is iterating through the lines of a file.

If you had a file and wanted to read it line by line, you'd write the following code:

```
file1 = open('filename.txt')
for lines in file1:
# do something
```

"Lines" is just the iterator variable for every string in file1, where each line is seen as an individual string and the file1 as the data set containing said strings. That's a convoluted explanation, but hopefully gets a question that you either have now or will have later squared away and neatly tucked off.

You're not restricted solely to data sets with for loops, though. Let's say you wanted to iterate through code 5 times, but didn't have a specific data set y ou were looping through. You could use the *range()* function to make that happen.

```
for i in range(5):
# do something
```

That code would run 5 times. If you wanted to count from 1 to 10 using for loops, you could do this:

```
for i in range(10):
print i+1 # i+1 because the computer starts
counting at 0
```

That's the bulk of what there is to know regarding for loops. Now, we've got to get into a topic that makes up literally every programming language and plays a huge part in any semi-sophisticated program.

CHAPTER 7

METHODS

Let's face it: you're going to have long programs. You're going to have programs which do a lot of things. You may have one chunk of code you have to reuse over and over to do this or that. Copying and pasting everything that you've got to utilize is going to be very unwieldy and altogether just very difficult to read for anybody who comes along and has to maintain your code (this includes the future version of you, who will inevitably look at code that the past you wrote and wonder what in the world you were actually trying to say.)

There's a way to fix this problem though. There's this magical little utility that Python provides - as does pretty much every programming language - called a *method*.

A brief explanation, because I'm pretty sure that I've said both at different times in this book: a function and a method are the same thing. Well, technically. Both refer to a set of code which optionally returns a value and can be called from within other methods/functions. *Function* is typically the term for these that would be used by C and C++ programmers. *Method* is the term used within object - oriented programming languages such as Python. There's no difference between the two, and if you mention a *function* to a Python programmer, you may get a funny look, but they'll know exactly what you mean. "Method" and "function" are interchangeable. Per habit, I call them function, and will probably do so throughout this chapter. Just know that function means method means function.

So let's look at how a method may be set up in C-style pseudocode.

```
main function
{ int x;
x = doSomething(3);
}
doSomething(int y)
{ // code here
return y;
}
```

Make any sense? Let's break this down.

The definition for a function across most languages is like this:

return data type **functionName**(*arguments*)
{ code
return value (if relevant, not all functions need to return a value)
}

So, for more pseudocode, let's say we wanted a function that accepted any number, and gave back to you that number multiplied by 3. How do you think we'd do that?

It'd look a bit like this:

```
multiplyNum(number)
{ return number * 3;
}
```

Then if we had a main function...

```
main {
x = multiplyNum(3);
}
```

Can you guess what x would be? If you guessed 3, then you're absolutely right. This may remind you a bit of the whole f(x) exercises from high school and college math.

Luckily, Python - as it does with most things - makes working with functions super -duper incredibly easy. You don't have to declare any given return type, you just kind of make the function. You don't have to specify the data types of the argument, they're implied by your code.

In order to declare a function in Python, here's all you have to do:

```
def functionName(arguments):
# code here
```

Simple, right?

Create a new file called ch7.py . We're goin g to be working with functions for a moment (how exciting).

Let's make a home square footage calculator. It's going to be super simple for our purposes and assume that every room is a perfect square, but it's a starting point.

The first thing we want to do is make a list to store all of our rooms' square footage. We don't know the size of any rooms yet, so let's just make it an empty list, like so:

```
rooms = []
```

Afterwards, we need to make a method to calculate area. What it's going to do is take the lengt h and width, then print the room square footage, then finally return that square footage. This will make more sense contextually within the main part of the program.

For now, just make the method.

```
def calculateArea(length, width):
print "\nRoom square footage: %d" % (length
* width)
return length * width
```

After that, we need a function which takes our list of room square footages and adds them together to return the total square footage of the house.

```
def addRooms(roomList):
sqft = 0
```

Now we have to iterate through the list:

```
for room in roomList:
```

Then we have to add whatever value "room" is to the total square footage variable (*sqft*).

```
sqft += room        # sqft = sqft + room
```

Then we just have to return the total square footage:

```
return sqft
```

Now we can get to the actual chunk of our program. How neat!

The first thing we want to do is ask how many rooms the house has. We're going to have to convert this to an integer data type, so we're going to get input, but we're also going to place the integer type cast wrapper around it. This is wordy, but here's what I mean:

```
roomCount = int(raw_input("How many
rooms does the house have? "))
```

Now, when the user puts in a number, it'll automatically be changed from a string to an int. There are more verbose ways of doing this, like this:

```
roomCount = raw_input("How many rooms does
the house have?")
int(roomCount)
```

But we just saved a fair amount of space and programming time and made prettier code, so what we did works super well.

Now we need to use that roomCount inte ger in order to iterate through a loop. With every iteration of this loop, we want to get the length of a room and the width of a room, then calculate the area of the room, then add the room to our *rooms* list. It's also important to not forget that since w e're dealing with *raw_input*, we have to cast these length and width variables to integers just like a second ago.

So first we have to declare our loop:

```
for i in range(roomCount):
```

Then we have to get the length and width:

```
length = int(raw_input("\nWhat is the length?
"))
width = int(raw_input("\nWhat is the width? "))
```

After that, we need to get the area from those two variables. We're going to send them to our calculateArea function. Since that function returns a value, we can store the result of the function to a variable. Following? Observe.

```
area = calculateArea(length, width)
```

Easy peasy. So next, we've got to add that to our list:

```
rooms.append(area)
```

If you're interested in more shortcuts, then we actually technically could have avoided creating an area variable at all. Since the *calculateArea* function returns a value, and the rooms.append function takes an argument of a value, we can just through the calculateArea function right into the rooms.append function:

```
rooms.append(calculateArea(length,width))
```

See how elegant that is? I'm going to change my code to that, actually. The only reason we did the other is to demonstrate that you can assign the return value of a function to a variable.

Anyway, after we've gone through all the rooms and calculated their square footage, we need to print out the total square footage. This is super easy. You know how we've been inserting values into formatted strings? Well, since addRooms() returns a value, we can just go ahead and do that!

```
print "\n\nTotal square footage is:\t%d"
% addRooms(rooms)
```

By the end, your code should look like this:

```
rooms = []
def calculateArea(length, width):
print "\nRoom square footage: %d" % (length
* width)
return length * width def
addRooms(roomList) : sqft
= 0
for room in roomList:
sqft += room
return sqft
roomCount = int(raw_input("How many rooms
does the house have? "))
```

39

```
for i in range(roomCount):
length = int(raw_input("\nWhat is the
length? "))
width = int(raw_input("\nWhat is the width?
")) rooms.append(calculateArea(length, width))
print "\n\nTotal square footage is:\t%d" %
addRooms(rooms)
```

Go ahead and save and test it out. If everything works out, then you've got yourself a full -fledged adding machine, my friend. That's cause for celebration in my eyes.

CHAPTER 8

FILE I/O

One of the most integral parts of programming is file input and output. This fundamental activity has so many varied uses that it's really impossible to pin down its usefulness in any mild sentiment. You can save progress, import and export data, do such a variety of things really that it's absurd.

File import and export is such an integral part of so many applications. Word processing, for example - every time you save or open a file, you're exporting or importing data. Every time that you save a video game, you 're exporting data about your current position in the game world, your current health and inventory, all of that. It's such a deeply useful system that it'd be nigh sacrilegious to somehow pass it up in the scope of this book.

What's more is that Python ma kes it incredibly easy. How cool is that? A lot of languages make it terribly complicated, but not Python, no sirree.

First, let's talk about opening a file.

Opening Files

Writing files is very straightforward in Python. Every interaction with a file, be it reading or writing or appending, in Python occurs through the open method. This method returns a *File* object, which can then be manipulated.

The open method is spectacularly well -rounded, as well as easy to use. It takes two variables: the file name, an d the interaction mode.

There are four main interaction modes you need to know about:

Operator	Meaning	Description
"w"	Write mode	Erases file, writes from scratch.
"r"	Read mode	Can only read file.
"r+"	Read/write mode	User must position self - can read/write.
"a"	Append mode	Adds content to an existing file.

You don't *have* to specify an interaction mode, however. If you fail to specify an interaction mode, it will default to the read-only mode.

The way to open a file is something along t he lines of this:

```
f = open("file.txt", "w")
```

Let's work with this a little bit. Go ahead and create a new file, call it ch8.py.

What we're going to do in this set of code is create a file that has numbers from one to ten. Simple enough, no?

The first thing we want to do in this file is create our file object variable. Just like a second ago, let's call it f. We're going to call our file *example.txt* and we're going to open it with write-only mode.

```
f = open("example.txt", "w")
```

Now we just have to make our l oop. In order to write to the file, we're going to use the file method *write()*, which accepts an argument of a formatted string.

```
for i in range(10):
    f.write("%d\n" % (i + 1))
```

Then, when we're done with a certain file, we always, always have to close it. Not doing so can lead to glitchy programs, resource leaks, and even corrupted files. Not a good set of things to have happen to your user. Let's just avoid that altogether. We close files by calling the *close()* method.

```
f.close()
```

By the end of it, your modest lil' chunk of code should look something like this:

```
f = open("example.txt",
"w") for i in range(10):
    f.write("%d\n" % (i + 1))
    f.close()
```

Save this and run it. In your sidebar on Atom, you should see a little file called example.txt open up. Click it an d view its contents. You should see the numbers 1 through 10! Perfect.

Now we're going to feed these back in using Python's interface for file reading. Below that chunk of code, we're going to open example.txt again, but this time, we're going to use read-only mode.

We're going to go ahead and open it again:

```
f = open("example.txt", "w")
```

Now, we want to go through it line by line. We talked about how exactly this works when we were talking about for loops earlier. That whole spiel about iterating through a file line-by-line remains relevant here. So let's do what we talked about earlier:

```
for line in f:
```

Easy enough, right? Now we're going to print the data from every line of the text file, but we're going to multiply it by 3. The first thing we have to do i s another integer cast, since every line read from the text file is read as a string. We'd do that like so:

```
line = int(line)
```

Now we're going to print line multiplied by 3.

```
print "%d" % (line * 3)
```

See? Super easy to do, super intuitive too. Last thing we 've got to do is close the file.

```
f.close()
```

Save the program and run it again. Your output should look very similar to this:

```
user@userpc:~/Python$ python
ch8.py 3 6 9 12 15 18 21 24
```

See how easy that all is? Python makes working with files an absolute cinch. It's really sort of impressive. Other languages tend to make it a tad more convoluted, but Python - per usual - comes around and makes the whole process incredibly easy.

So, we've talked a bit about how the variable f was a "file object". But what does object really mean?

That's the kind of question that we're going to tackle in the upcoming chapter.

CHAPTER 9

OOP FUNDAMENTALS

Back in the day, programming was a lot less straightforward than it is today. The modus operandi used to be something called procedural programming, which meant that your program just ran, start to end, with very little room to change or modify it overtime, and it was often easier to just write your code all over using some of the logic from the previous set of code than to rework the code that you already had. Making one or two changes had the possibility to create a number of issues in your program that would take seemingly forever in order to fix.

This all changed when the concept of object -oriented programming came along. The charge was led by a language called Ada, named after Ada Lovelace, one of the mothers of modern computing. In the 80s, the procedural language C was updated by a guy named Bjarne Stroustrup to add classes, which we'll get to momentarily. This was a h uge part in the shift towards object oriented programming. C++ was actually a bit of a bridge, as it allowed for both the procedural and the object-oriented paradigms. Then along came a little language you may have heard of called Java. Java was, for lack of a better term, an absolute game changer. There's a reason that Oracle, the company which created and maintained Java (then known as Sun), is worth billions today.

Java caught on for a few reasons. The first of these is that it was extremely portable. It ran within a virtual machine and was an interpreted language as opposed to a compiled language, which meant that there was a lot of abstraction between Java and the lower levels of the machine. It also meant that a code written on a Windows system could be run on a Macintosh, Unix, or Linux system. Writing in Java enabled your code to reach a lot more people.

The second reason is because it was the first programming language to allow much interactivity with webpages. Scripting languages had hardly been de veloped, so Java was often embedded into webpages. This use occasionally fell to the wayside after the development of ECMAScript/JavaScript, and has fallen to the wayside even moreso with the development of other languages like Python, Ruby, and Lua. Regardless, for its time in the embryonic world wide web, it was a huge deal.

The other reason is that it was the first major language to solely support an object-oriented paradigm. Everything was contained within a class, no matter what. Pieces of programs were much easier to bind together than ever before, and it all around was just a huge step forward for making programming less esoteric and more approachable and less time-intensive.

So what is object-oriented programming exactly? We'll get into the specific concepts underlying object-oriented programming in the next chapter, but it's all based around the idea of classes and objects.

A **class** is a concept which is made up a lot of little characteristics. For this chapter and the next, we're going to go ahead and use cars as our example. A *car* could be an example of a class. Every car has doors, windows, a windshield, and a horn. A class is a way of putting all these little pieces of data and these functions together into one package.

An **object** is an *instance* of a class. What this means is that Car may be the broad concept, but my car and my friend's car are two different *instances* of this.

Understanding how classes are built and what exactly goes into them makes a tad more sense when you see how a class is declared in Python.

Every class definition in Python is like this:

```
class className(parent
class): def init ():
relevant class variables
```

We'll talk about parent classes in the next chapter, but for right now, all you need to know is that every class which isn't derived from another class has *object* in place of their parent class.

So let's say we wanted to make a vehicle class. What do all vehicles have in common? They all have doors. They have a make and model. They have a production year. They all have a horn. They all either have air conditioning or they don't, which could be a boolean variable. That's a decent enough place to start.

Let's go ahead and define our vehicle class to start:

```
def Vehicle(object):
```

Alright, so now we need to talk about initializer f unctions before we make them. Initializer functions are used whenever you create a new instance of an object. Remember how we created an instance of the *file* object earlier and gave it the variables *filename* and *interaction-mode*? This works similarly. We can have it so that we actually send arguments when we defined a version of the object.

So let's look at the variables we talked about:

- doors
- make, model
- production year
- air conditioning

We can throw those in our initializer function and have them defined for each instance of the class. We're also going to assume we're working only with 4 -door cars for now, because I have a point to make here in a few paragraphs. Anyway, let's start add the arguments for make/model, production year, and air conditioning to our initializer function, and actually code the thing. We also have to add the *self* argument first and foremost, because, well, Python. The exact reasoning is beyond the scope of this book.

```
def __init__(self, makeAndModel, prodYear,
airConditioning):
```

Now here's what we do:

```
self.makeAndModel = makeAndModel
self.prodYear = prodYear
self.airConditioning =
airConditioning self.doors = 4
```

The first three take arguments defined when the object is created, and the last one is defined by default. Good stuff, super easy.

Now, before we finish up this class, let's add a cute little method called "honk" which just prints out the phrase "honk honk!".

With every class function, you have to give self as an argument:

def honk(self):

After that, we just have to print what we want to print:

```
print "%s says: Honk! Honk!"
% self.makeAndModel
```

Now let's go into our main code and test this out. Make a new instance of the vehicle class. Mine will be a 2004 Pontiac Grand Am.

```
grandAm = Vehicle("Pontiac Grand Am", 2004,
True)
```

There we go. Now you have an instance of your own class! Woo! Let's test that this works by calling the Vehicle method "honk" right below our object declaration:

```
grandAm.honk()
```

Save this and run. It should go pretty flawlessly and print out exactly what we expect it to.

But let's say we had a sporty Grand Am, and it only had 2 doors? What could we do?

This is very simple. Just access the grandAm object's *doors* variable and set it to 4.

```
grandAm.doors = 2
```

Now test this by printing it out:

```
print "My car has %d doors." % grandAm.doors
```

Everything go well? Fantastic. In the next chapter, we're going to build on these a bit, but we'll mainly be talking about bigger OOP concepts.

CHAPTER 10

DEEPER INTO OOP

So we've made it this far, all the way to the l ast chapter. Man. That's pretty awesome. There are just a few more things we need to talk about before we wrap this book up. We're going to look at the four concepts of object -oriented programming and how they apply to Python.

Inheritance

The first major concept is called "inheritance". This refers to things being able to derive from another. Let's take sports cars for instance. All sports cars are vehicles, but not all vehicles are sports cars. Moreover, all sedans are vehicles, but all vehicles are not sedans, and sedans are *certainly* not sports cars, even though they're both vehicles.

So basically, this concept of Object -Oriented programming says that things can and should be chopped up into as small and fine of precise of concepts as possible.

In Python, this is done by deriving classes.

Let's say we had another class called SportsCar. Create a new file called ch10.py and recreate the car class from the last chapter.

```
class Vehicle(object):
def __init__(self, makeAndModel, prodYear,
airConditioning):
self.makeAndModel = makeAndModel
```

```
self.prodYear = prodYear
self.airConditioning =
airConditioning self.doors = 4
def honk(self):
print "%s says: Honk! Honk!"
% self.makeAndModel
```

Now, below that, create a new class called SportsCar, but instead of deriving *object*, we're going to derive from Vehicle.

```
class SportsCar(Vehicle)
def init (self, makeAndModel, prodYear,
airConditioning):
self.makeAndModel = makeAndModel
self.prodYear = prodYear
self.airConditioning =
airConditioning self.doors = 4
```

Leave out the honk function, we only need the constructor function here. Now declare a sports car. I'm just going to go with the Laferrari.

```
ferrari = SportsCar("Ferrari Laferrari",
2016, True)
```

Awesome. Now test this by calling

```
ferrari.honk()
```

and then saving and running. It should go off without a hitch.

Why is this? This is because the notion of inheritance says that a child class derives functions and class variables from a parent class. Easy enough concept to grasp. The next one is a little tougher.

Polymorphism

The idea of polymorphism is that the same process can be performed in different ways depending upon the needs of the situation. This can be done in two different ways in Python: *method overloading*, and *method overriding*.

Method overloading is defining the same function twice with different arguments. For example, we could give two different initializer functions to our Vehicle class. Right now, it just assumes a vehicle has 4 doors. If we wanted to specifically say how many doors a car had, we could make a new initializer function below our current one with an added *doors* argument, like so (the newer one is on the bottom):

```
def __init__(self, makeAndModel, prodYear,
airConditioning):
self.makeAndModel = makeAndModel
self.prodYear = prodYear
self.airConditioning = airConditioning
self.doors = 4
def __init__(self, makeAndModel, prodYear,
airConditioning, doors):
self.makeAndModel = makeAndModel
self.prodYear = prodYear
self.airConditioning =
airConditioning self.doors = doors
```

Somebody now when creating an instance of the Vehicle class can *choose* whether they define the number of doors or not. If they don't, the number of doors is assumed to be 4.

Method overriding is when a child class *overrides* a parent class's function with its own code.

To illustrate, create another class which extends Vehicle called Moped. Set the doors to 0, because that's absurd, and set air conditioning to false. The only relevant arguments are make/model and production year. It should look like this:

```
class Moped(Vehicle):
def __init__(self, makeAndModel, prodYear):
self.makeAndModel =
makeAndModel self.prodYear =
prodYear self.airConditioning =
False self.doors = 0
```

Now, if we made an instance of the Moped class and called the honk() method, it would honk. But it's common knowledge that mopeds don't honk, they beep. So let's override the parent class's honk method with our own. This is super simple. We just redefine the function in the child class:

```
def honk(self):
print "%s says: Beep! Beep!"
% self.makeAndModel
```

I'm part of the 299,000,000 Americans who couldn't name a make and model of moped if their life depended on it, but you can test out if this works for yourself but declaring an instance of the Moped class and trying it out.

Abstraction

The next major concept in obje ct-oriented programming is *abstraction*. This is the notion that the programmer and user should be far from the inner workings of the computer. This has two benefits.

The first is that it decreases the inherent security risks and the possibility for catastrophic system errors, by either human or otherwise. By abstracting the programmer from the inner workings of the computer like memory and the CPU and often even the operating system, there's a low chance of any sort of mishap causing irreversible damage.

The second is that the abstraction innately makes the language easier to understand, read, and learn. Though it makes the language a tad bit less powerful by taking away some of the power that the user has over the entire computer architecture, this is traded instead for the ability to program quickly and efficiently in the language, not wasting time dealing with trivialities like memory addresses or things of the like.

These apply in Python because, well, it's incredibly simple. You can't really get down int o the nitty gritty of the computer, or do much with memory allocation or even specifically allocate an array size too easily, but this is a tradeoff for amazing readability, a highly secure language in a highly secure environment, and ease of use with programming. Compare the following snippet of code from C:

```
#include <stdio.h>
int main(void) {
printf("hello
world"); return 0;
}
```

to the Python code for doing the same:

```
print "hello world"
# That's it. That's all there is to it.
```

Abstraction is generally a net positive for a large number of applications that are being written today, and there's a reason Python and other object-oriented programming languages are incredibly popular.

Encapsulation

The last major concept in object -oriented programming is that of encapsulation. This one's the easiest to explain. This is the notion that common data should be put together, and that code should be modular. I'm not going to spend long explaining this because it's a super simple concept. The entire notion of classes is as concise of an example as you can get for encapsulation: common traits and methods are bonded together under one cohesive structure, making it super easy to create things of the sort without having to create a ton of super specific variables f or every instance.

CONCLUSION

Welp, there we go. We finally made it to the end of our little Python adventure. First, I'd like to say thank you for making it through to the end of *Python for Beginners: The Ultimate Guide to Python Programming*. Let's hope it was informative and able to provide you with all of the tools you need to achieve your goals, whatever they may be.

The next step is to use this knowledge. Whether it be as a hobby or as a career move, by learning the basics of Python, you just made one of the best decisions of your life, and your goal now should be finding ways to use it in your day -to-day life to make life easier or to accomplish things you've wanted to accomplish for a long while.

Finally, if you found this book useful in any way, a review on Amazon is always appreciated!

DESCRIPTION

There are few better pursuits you could undertake than learning to program. Not many things will benefit you as directly as programming will. This book will teach you how to go from setting up your Python environment to working with complex object-oriented concepts, all in a matter of no time. If you want to learn Python quickly but still have an impressive grasp on it, this just might be the book for you.

If you're on the edge of learning Python, I sh ould just say that programming is the only form of self -expression that allows the end user to directly interact with your art. Programming is a science, but it's also an art. In this book, you're going to learn how to start to use this hugely dynamic language in order to make computers do what you want them to do.

Whether you're learning to program as a career move, as a hobbyist, or as somebody just looking to dabble in computer programming, learning programming is ultimately one of the best moves you'll ever make for yourself. It's my goal in this book to ensure that you are an able Python programmer in no time at all. There are many books about Python programming on the market, but there are few that will cater so kindly to helping you get on your feet i n Python and helping you feel like you know the language inside and out in no time at all. This is one of them.